ZACH JACKSON

Chandelier

Broken Sleep Books
brokensleepbooks.com

All rights reserved; no part of this chapbook
may be reproduced by any means
without the publisher's permission.

Published 2019,
Broken Sleep Books:
Carmarthenshire, Wales

brokensleepbooks.com

Zach Jackson has asserted his right to
be identified as the author of this
Work in accordance with:
the Copyright, Designs and Patents Act 1988

First Edition

Lay out your unrest.

Publisher/Editor: Aaron Kent
Editor: Charlie Baylis

Typeset in UK by Aaron Kent

Broken Sleep Books is committed to
a sustainable future for our planet,
and therefore uses print on
demand publication.

brokensleepbooks@gmail.com

ISBN: 9781794597778

Contents

Crucible	7
A Death	8
Lottery	9
Hecatombs	12
Top Heavy	13
Florist	14
Feeding Thunder	16
Midas	18
Lunar Sketches	19
Hylas and the Nymphs	23
The Gilling Sword	25
Moonbathers	26
Down from the Falls	27
Eazyzap 4000	29
For the Soul of Your Mother	30
Erasure	31
Engines	33
Exam	34
Morgue	35
Birth of a Star	36
Dull	38
Dr. Joseph-Ignace Guillotin	39
Bookshelf	40
The Anaesthetists	42
Flamenco Dancer on Station Road	43
Oath	45
And the Bad Poets	46
One Last Drink	47

Meteorite   48
Stillborn   49
The Size of a Human Heart   50

Acknowledgements   53

CHANDELIER

For the calm after the storm
and the dark spots in my vision.
For Eleanor

Crucible
For Rhi

The way the sun
elongates over a lake at twilight
the 2 watt halogen energy saver
achieves on your
closed eyelids
after about a minute or so's warm up,
a timemachine whir,
and a strobe of blinks.
When you open your eyes
I see this landscape roll halfway
into your skull, nearing brain,
but not touching,
revealing the cavern
networks of your iris;
a staggered echo
sounding back my own voice
from the crucible of your gaze:

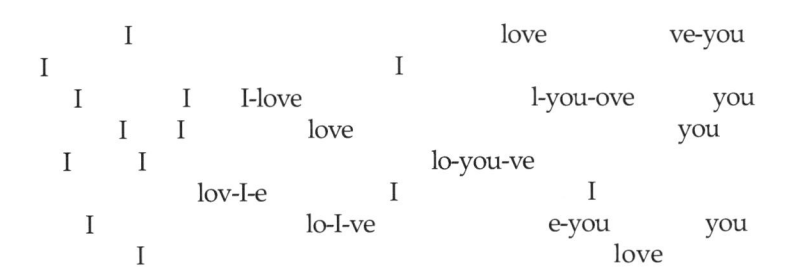

```
            I                              love         ve-you
I                               I
    I         I   I-love                 l-you-ove        you
        I    I            love                            you
    I    I                         lo-you-ve
              lov-I-e          I              I
    I                  lo-I-ve            e-you        you
         I                                     love
```

A Death

Inside the beacon,
someone found the blue eyed lamb hung,
throat frilled as gunny sack,
sea-cold
in the first field of the coming sun.

Atlas and axis disengaged.
Both strung and trapper.
Music of death-rattle.
Selena's tracks between
used rubbers and chocolate wrappers.

How many nights before death
caught in mooring rope?
The stars washed in so low
a tall man might knock his head,
the moon stooped enough to hang his coat.

Lottery

The numbers came that day
                         and that night
    I walked out upon the blued snakes
                      and the pied stockinged sky
    showed me great hellish hullabaloos
of the zodiac
but no rungs   and the cunt-
mauve
    recently   deceased
sun
must have maggots worming
    new   ways
through its droop
                         Eyed cancer/pissed darkness
    I held an owl
    against a brick-front house screaming
I didn't lose the lottery, motherfucker.
I just bought a bookmark.

The inferno ain't circles
The crackling red mosques of Dis
Their bells rattle my bones
The infernal Goddesses
patrol my veins.

I am the shape of hell
    for IiiiiiIIIIi... yiiyyou
    I have authored a devil
in me
to cull in me
to   lace these boots with rainbows and wade the bogs   to
                         Breathe smoke in the cryogeny
Break dismal syntax
of existing as
abomination
To slow the sums

Rot is the simplification of complex matter
                                          There is no nakedness
        as the nakedness
of decomposition

I have seen it

w < [are ([i] -possible (x) - equa [y], tion), s]
.e   m

e x p a n   d   i   n   g

In the exam hall even the light's construction lines through the torn, used-to-be-red curtains take on the dryness of the room like a passenger that won't shut the fuck up about the holidaybabydecorweathersportgovernmentnewipad and all the calculators read 3(]1)1^5.

A soldier's work is algebraic/great un-dressers

                              and great drinkers
Tonight-

Hair of the dog that ripped your guts into the street
and bolted with them like a chain of Richmonds.

The plantigrades marched home
                        and I crawl

not like
babies
alligators
                            I bit the gorgon
        headed night
                            and death-rolled
        the universe dead
for starting with me.

Death is ever so big
for civvies

I thought
but it could fit
in
a hatbox a bracketed
hypothetical (   )

DO NOT try to mine the night for a star
the pick-axed raspberry
burrs lacerate little vessels
in your throat

                    and your belly will slosh with blood
      like a leather zahato
      lashed to a thirsty mule.
              and you will come to know
     above all else

The ghosts pulled through a cigarette

Gods come around second hand

The heartless mathematic of death.

Hecatombs
For the deciduous boys of Richmond

Vicious saints
in sallowed plumes,
fragments of tibia,
blooms of apricot

Gather young like kindling
for the pyre;
the sunless halls
of bisected Osiris.

Rag and bone seraphim
of His valvular gates,
golden throated,
eat souls like grapes.

Top Heavy
For Spruce

You fell so often
your skull developed craters
and was moonish,
fizzing lunar transients.

Grit asteroids revised
your cranial map.

Maria flowered darkly.

Mountains surged from plate faults
and basaltic valleys whirled beside
your blood orogeny.

The sun dripped away
behind your swell of horns
and lit you- a theatre
of bones

        perched on the ridge of the astrobleme
                ahent the convie,
kicking your feet.

And
 I sat beside you
       eating moonlight
               sweet from knives

                            then
                                dissolved
                                          into

orbit.

Florist

The sun,
guillotined due-west
where land and sky conspire,
dilates,
making prodigal the clouds
with hems of sugared raspberry,
and they gather and fortify
into great bouquets of carnations.

Makes the nun in you
blaspheme and grip
tight on your crucifix,
unsure of a visitation
by Devil or God
rearranging your insides
like a great old maid
fluffing a pillow.

Makes you
thumb clumsy
for what's left
of your soul,
fold it for an airplane
and sail it foxed and spotted
into the arrangement
screaming
save yourself.

You were never really sure
what it was,
or if it was there,
but you learnt
by the way it dies
something was
and you can tell now.

It's small
but unvanquished.
Fluted like a cobra
from wicker; fumes
in an empty tank

and I feel my thorns clipped
lovingly to the soil

while the floristry of the sun
wilts into aubergine
sulk of evening,
achromatic midnight.

Feeding Thunder

Thunder mews from shantung
hems, damask, moire,
raw silk.

She peeps from the underworld
of the drapery
with eyes like button slips,
drives a flank
against my shin
and prowls the stairway.

Our language is bent
into bare essentials.
Almost entirely

sweet sucking: tuhtuhtuh
whistling sibilance: psspsspss

All we need.

We could very well live in dead silence
unfound by murder or charity.

There is something
McCarthian in the quiet.

Something apocalyptic,
core;

older than our age combined.

Ancient compounds
of dirt-basic peace
engorge
the vowels of her hunger.

They flick
from my consonants
in thick wet droplets.

I give our signal
and follow to the bowl,
watching her four-beat gait.

Either side the pit
where treatments are administered,
scapula thread-
twin orcas breathing,
diving, and every four yards
she executes dreadful Orphic turns.

Be calm, beast.
I am here

unwon by Hades.

     All we need.

Midas

Explin thissen feeal mornin'
Lowsy w'faieerieland motes
N' syhroopy, uthaahr
Eyeed thruh't fith o' whisky.
Thy alchemy transmutin'
Dayzeez t'bu'ercups
'N' dogrorses t' liuns.

Spek pookish autumn!
C'lectin' thy culluh fee.

Thy sundowns lollin' on't hryzun
Like fresh sevid 'eds
Muckyin t' place up,
Anowihs-
Mornin' yelluh
As thy leaf.

'N' us flayt 'ands not knuhwin'
T'applaud ooer preay.

Lunar Sketches
For Luke

Newcastle: Mouth washed out with soap.

Cornsilk crook of a mother's elbow
holding her portion of dark;
her slick and sleeping infant.

Cheltenham: Six teeth out.

Bent and still as a surgeon over a patient.
Sclera-white with fractals of spun mercury;
burst vessels of wolf-silver blood
scatter in ever fraying glassy bolts.
Anaesthetic awareness-
the blade coming down.
I can say nothing.

Swanpool

A resurrection!
Miraculous to be sure.
O pale face of Ophelia
sailing in the lake,
clenching poppies and rue
daisy chained, when
a cosmonaut moorhen
crossing the whole surface
defibrillates
and warbles her into new life.
Her song like a sonar ping
stretched, processed for words
and melody, resumes
its lunatic wonder. Death?
A simple luftpause.

Pink Moon

In absentia

Kutna Hora

Wraithlike
over the bone chapel
and the blooming, orchidish
chandelier of human remains.
Macerated toxic-blue
like a smoke ring from a cigarette
lined with mercury.

Gilling West: In storm's clearing.

In autumn, when sun's light
turns onto a spool,
and wind flits the scarlet
maple like a bloody cape,
there! Inextricable
from a sky-shatter of branchlets;
a burlesque fix of leaves,
wiping a dagger off,
turning light onto its waist
and growing gravid,
phasing gibbous.

Cwmtwrch: Solstice.

Bromine and dead lamb's wool
stained and twisted in the black dyke
where eggs of spume giddy
with tallow.
Investigate with a stick and see
words ooze like pus,
and squirming maggots of old light.

St. Ives: Drinking tinnies on the beach.

Reaching delicately almost full circle
around a worn bombazine heart-
a necklace's clasp.
Dragline silk, bloodless husk.

Super Moon

Molecular structure of a psychic tear
as viewed through a powerful microscope.

Richmond: Time at the bar.

Borax-matte ashtray
to stub your glance,
with a murky aureole
the colour of burning acetate.
The cinema of the sky
shrivelling into the flames
like flowers blooming backwards.

Stock Screensaver

Crushed buttercup lucine
in cindery Reynisfjara,
beneath the titanic enmity
of Miyrdajaskyl and Katla.

Easby Abbey

Monkish, early, low.
Small enough looking
to have popped up
via one of our sooty lums
with a nightjar nest for a pillbox hat
and a bloody phlegm
of looks-like-grizzlies cloud
on its weak complexion.
Fit nicely in the pit of your collar;
in a pocket and cause hardly a lump.

Kotor

Constant and vital as a crucifix
high on a wall,
in that if it were taken down
a clean disk of virgin darkness
above ebony furnitures
dusty with stars and dead skin
would show us heartless,
mathless blackness.

Channel: Night ferry.

Holm;
sweet drogue scooping pink
lemonade, slowing the prow
of the earth to a sleepy, sea-murmured
nod.

Albany Place: Sea facing balcony.

Pigmented linseed oil
picked from the nail folds
of a sunset painter- lintish.

Pen-Y-Cae: Witching Hour.

Fit to roll down the black mountain.
Leaves silver splinters
in your look so you might turn
to a clock and fail to read the time.
Not worn by the night
but wearing it-
a cwellere's hood
whispering over our small hemisphere,
"There never was a new black".

Hylas and the Nymphs

Libidinous silence
whistles from the rim
of an empty amphora.
Dracula white
bodies almost
light giving with
new wound lips. Index
knuckle grazing navel
and descending.
Crocodilian sisters
drag through rhizome
forests. Yellow lilies burn
cold as honeymoons
in nights of hair.
Flat line sounds
in the ear. *Her cold
chest.* Glugging
euphoria reaching
temples.
Styx-black depths
heal a skin over.
Her cold lips.
Empty amphora.
Lungs drink black.
Cold tympanic
ecstasy curls
in grim borealis.
Violet light sings down—
a sedative.
Before dreams begin
middle toe noses
zygomatic, eels cattail.
Heel glides over
razorous shin.
Ribs pierce all seven

layers of skin.
No blood smokes.
Her lips,
not so cold as they were,
unseal our kiss. Spitting
feathers, the half God
waits.

The Gilling Sword

It wuruh bairn saw
That skimmer in
The myki kambre
Down bekkr.
A skellered blade,
Happ marking a grave
Since thee flytja
To our tveit,
Rifa skyr in thrithings
And loose, having
Liggja thi silver hilt
In our flow
With thi words
And diphthongs
Hammered to a pure,
Flat vowel.

Moonbathers

Dusk brews like strong forgotten tea,
rust through epiphanic puce,
turning the mind like a coin
over a bloody knuckle,
electrifying the carnival
of the zodiac.
Darknesses sublimated
through tiny
pores of sun wrack
our body's outline
indefinite as ghosts
are indefinite.
Stains us like paper.
There are scars we give ourselves
lit like galaxies
come evening,
and there are secret dens
the wet nose of the moon can't nuzzle
tucked behind our heads
like a tombstone.
We think of our skin
pleating between our ribs
like the fingers of a careful tailor,
and the floating bones
brought softly to the spine
as though presented at the feet
of an emperor;
or set carefully adrift
like white lily heads
on the surface of a jet
black stream. Breathing
out histories, futures
smoke from us
like heat from a fresh kill.
Arms in an X,
our eyes chime like spoons
stirring starlight into a cup.

Down From the Falls

Night

The night air through the willow,
sensual, quick
reminiscence of arrows;
a death-threat whispered
in the ear so close and low

it tickles. The prey stumbles.
Moon gluts the river
with unicorn blood
and buzzsaws of silver
break from the umbles,

tool black into ribbons,
corseting the hills
eventually to the opioid sea
perfect for circular flat
moons and suns

skimmed and sunk
childishly. Under the bridge
the corpse leaks nebulas
into the water, horn
sawn to a smooth sparkling stump.

Day

Leaves wink and greenly glow
like coins on a dancer's hip
while silent tension-breaks
of spun sugar sun
spangle rainbow

trout sired perturbations,
sharp as piano wire.
Kalashnikov locusts
empty out beneath
whitethroat incantations-

chur and yip. Deep
in portal shadow
of reflected water
the land moves
like a simple sheet

hung to dry.
Under a drowned dragon-
fly's snapped blue agate
a sharp of gneiss pierces the veil;
Odin's deposited eye.

Eazyzap 4000

Deepfreeze angel strip joint if you like.
Slow erasing exo-skeleton
tease until all that's left
are the crinoline beams,
and wings like keratin.

One by one,
sometimes two at a time
customers become
new dancers

stuck to the bars.
Small shopping bags
of electrons

dancing down lightning rods,
exploding, enlisting

in Icarian company.

For the Soul of Your Mother

An evil of colour
this sundown,
bedraggled with cloud-rips.
Lost I'd say, or left behind-
red-sided
garter snake ecdysis;
vixen smeared
over an oily road;
that thrift shop cardie
you'd never wear,
but for the soul of your mother,
can't take your eye off.

Erasure

The image of you in my head
is fraying,
tailing into anemone fire.
Your crisp lines jittered like
sutures on a skull.

Never just one burial ground.
The rot happens
in that Manchester grave
and the head.

First,
there is this Picassion mutation,
a steady morph
then acid baths,
and I'm left with:

Objects- colouring books,
foot operated
ash tray, pocket knife.

Details- a comfy femur,
your elbow bend
on the arm of the chair
I could express
mathematically with triangles
and degrees on squared
note paper.

Sense memory-
voice that soothes my mother,
voice-
god of my god,
smell of stew,
luminosity.

Bigger things-
warmth and awe,
cloudish serenity.

And I wish it hadn't taken
so long to admit,
but it's okay.

You dismantle,
patch after patch blacked out
over time
in the primordial alluvium
of thought,

and I'm left with
the raw materials.

The sweet erasure
poem of your soul.

Engines

Dry laughter of night trains—
beneath scoliotic spines of galaxies,
and moonlight rib bone stark around the boiler—
nips the ghosts of idle machines. The chains
holding cold engines have no weakness.
In neat cryogenic sleep dreaming of breath
their tidiness evokes emptiness;
emptiness imitates death.

Exam

Cloud-shift-

darkness dragged
like a gown
over a knife.

The moorlands brown
in a coping of sun,
cute as lemon twigs.

The watcher moves
its invigilation
haunt-slow down
fire scared
slopes. Its faux night
befuddling winchats,
pitting in dips, damping
plutonium glow of spaghnum
moss. Bog asphodel
less like stars now
than one watt filaments.

The sparked peaks
spitting snipes,
passing fen
wool like folded
notes.

Morgue

Five
metal
counters
spaced
along
the wintry room.
A square of blinding light
beaming down
on each one
like last chance
portals
to the next plane,
and ghosts,
like moths,
thrash at the bulbs.

Birth of a Star
For Sam

Imbibe the whisky
like it cures
what ails,

```
            l
         l
      i
    p
 S
```
```
       s
      e
      v
     l
      e
     s
    r
   u
   o
   y

   k
   c
   a
   b
```

and engage the dredged bay
of planktonic burners

suspended like dead insects
in a swimming pool.

Pick a gory one,
and evil eye the prick
until your lashes cage,
until focus dies.

And measure
in your scope
flawless mitosis.

Two stars from one,
burning
in the cindery gather.

Dull

I'd write in the dark so my partner could sleep
and the flies and moths and gnats and all three fucking
wise men
came in from great journeys
through the window
gathering in a starry way
between me and the screen
like lures of fishermen
asleep in fold out chairs-
tobacco black
and cold in their pipes-
and I'd swallow all their hooks
hoping one might pull
some fresh- squirming, lively
thing- but nothing came-
and they'd go away
to brighter things:
Leonine dreams
blustering a mane around her head.
The moon on the glass
like an LED standby.

Dr. Joseph-Ignace Guillotin

In a hotel room wake
as dawn drops
the moon
like a dinner plate,
and
from the slit
between the curtains
hazy mists of morning light
coast in
like blood from a wound
underwater.

All the birds and sharks
have started
to sing.

Bookshelf

The frosted luminosity
of a glass lamp

about the wattage of a smile
curled across

tender spectra of old leather
as if a rainbow was a beast

you could ride, kill,
skin, wear and eat,

zombies names
into neon monikers

of nightclubs.
Sunset strip of words,

The seeds of pyxidium
men and women

waiting for fertile soil.
Recently reads

carried like caskets
on the tops of the ordered

to a grave that never comes.
Their world is full

of this grim patience,
haunted by sticker ghosts

laughing exorcists
out the window,

rattling library chains.
Sextodecimo lean

like children bored at a funeral,
bitter, not at death,

but having to polish their
least comfy pair of shoes

and further still, wear them.
Fighting off dreams like a pack of dogs

I wait for a coffin to shake
or a pallbearer to die

while the grave, for me,
already darkly

hollows.

The Anaesthetists

Sing, sing anaesthesia from draw, cache, niche;
softer than sleep,

and we'll graze on the dusk clouds
out against the sky as though spread with a butter knife,
                                        sunned vermillion,
our neon jaws
flagged with photons.

Draconic exhalations of crushed jade
and orange peel rumble in the death-belly of stasis.
                                      High cerulean
notes have no shepherd;
the hours, no captain.

Dream-wreathed larks swim
neurone prairies; beds of electric. Bodies of silence throb
                                            eyelid alizarin.

What buds and hands unfurl in the cirrus gardens?
How dark the spalted oak with pattern or prophesy?

Sing! Sing plastic flowers into the void.
Cast the lotus eater's iris
                                      stormless viridian.

Flamenco Dancer on Station Road

A Mars storm
slim garnet cyclone

havocking
through automatic

doors our eyes
like weather chasers

trace patterns
craving a deeper

knowledge of
a wild formula

a nova
sun's last dramatics.

Poppy seed
black hair in bunches

should urchin
splay detonate should

as from palms
of a gardener

scatter free
and grow a tangle

in our salt
shakers and oolong.

The life her
small hands flick into

the ruffles
of muleta red

blood spill skirt
is ventriloquistic

a language
goading all the bulls

of the room.
Ligaments protrude

from the flutes
of her wrists tearing

and pleating
her garment into

zinnia-
for just ten minutes

of the day
our workload ignored.

Oath

A broken arch of rainbow
crumbles into raw azure
like some ancient Hellenic ruin
and I swear it
on my Great Grandfather's
Daughter's Grandson's grave.
From this nameless
complex
in summer's clearing,
            watch the unmoored seed
of a cottonwood tree drift a quarter mile
if your eyes and patience are good,
            and a sparrow clear till the e   a   r
                                                    t
                                                      h
                                                        c
                                                         u
                    .   r
                    .   v
                      .   e
                        .   s
                                        .

And the Bad Poets

And the bad poets-
perhaps not bad,
but uninspired,
write about
how we're beautiful
because we're all made of stars.
And I think
you stone cold
fucking prodigy,
you marvel,
you bright shining son of a bitch.

Only a brilliant genius
could turn the stars ugly.

One Last Drink

Ah, late is the hour
and wide swing satellites
in digital sky.

God's flicked cigarettes,
and living broidery of the moon
slicked in the thick sickly
oils of naked night.

One last drink
to the milky eye rock,
blind but never lost.
The man in the moon
blows out suns
like they were dandelion clocks.

Meteorite

Our ancestors would call this an omen
and sacrifices would be made.
The quick green dart fertilising blood ovums
in the dirt as it passed.

Immolated mantis
stoppered in a beer bottle
hucked by a violent forgetful drunk
in the black churchy vaults
of mesosphere.

In the field
the foxes' patina.
A rack of deer on the mountain
still and greened as pond statues.
The alien rent up
in the curvature
of their frightened eyes,
breaking,
expiring,

burning a shade
that betrays the materials
of which it is made.

This is the art of death

holding not a scythe
but a brush,

not a grudge
but a pallet.

Stillborn

One morning
after sorting through
the glass and plastic,
they found you
woven through the general waste.

A dread-pearl
in a red bloom
fading out to sunset's
peach-fire

on a calyx of tissue,
newspaper, and half rot
suspended above still pools.

Your tiny machinery
softly visible
through bluish skin.

Vein lattice, leaf
bones, and pea heart.
All you were given
folded and pinched,
origami simple;

a Brechtian cherub
bearing stopped clockwork
from a poinsettia stain-

the stage-hands in revolt.

The Size of a Human Heart
For Ben

If a black hole
passed through the Oort cloud
we wouldn't notice,
not at first.

There'd be comets,
the outer orbitals disturbed,
a lensing effect on distant celestials-
nothing fatal.

Making its way
into the solar system,
gas giants drag
into an accretion disk;
a super heated
murder halo.
              We'd see this.

Jupiter unravelling
like a knot of yarn.
Hydrogen and helium
drawn from the skein,

and sweet benzene.
Even the sun eventually would spill
for the formidable broth.

And at the end of if it all

your heart,
your whole brave heart
would be the only thing
jutting from the singularity,

defying all scientific reason
again.

Acknowledgements

If reading begins with the death of the author, then call a priest, give Cash his tools, get the florist to work- I prefer lilies. If someone said, "Keep this to yourself or swim with the fishes", I'd say, "Pass the fucking snorkel". If this is it, I humbly accept my fate. Rest In Poesy! But there are things, certain special things; utterly spinal things. Things that make the author.

Things that must be, at this juncture, resuscitated, to live a long and happy life on some back-brain promenade of your mind.

The survivors are as follows:
My family for believing in me so fervently it often makes me nauseous.
Helen and John Phillips for giving me the home in which the bulk of these words were written.
Aaron Kent and Charlie Baylis of Broken Sleep who tolerated my incessant edits with patience and understanding.
My friends and any strangers that tolerated my rambling about poetry while drunk or otherwise.
And, Rhiannon, who makes being me worth the bother.

LAY OUT YOUR UNREST

Printed in Poland
by Amazon Fulfillment
Poland Sp. z o.o., Wrocław